Luke (Spiderman),
& Claire —
Don't forget
to walk him
every day!

Ryan Nusbickel

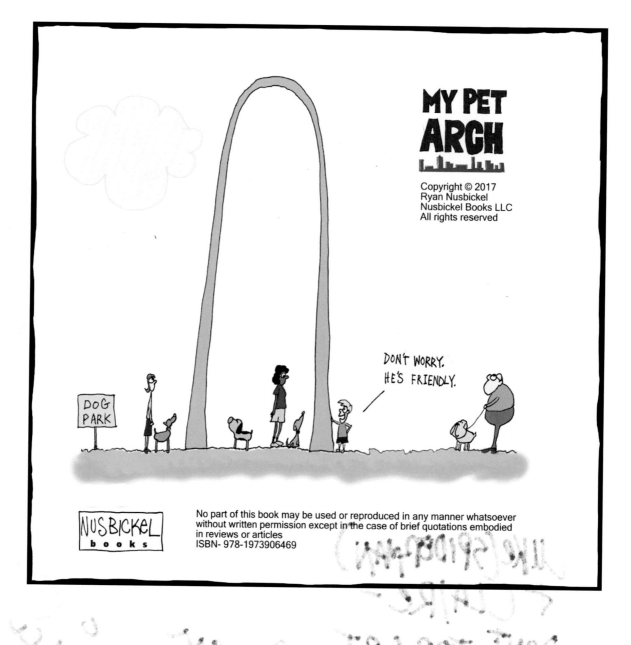

MY PET ARCH

Copyright © 2017
Ryan Nusbickel
Nusbickel Books LLC

NUSBICKEL books

ISBN- 978-1973906469

For Margaret and the girls, who put up with my tall tales on a daily basis.

The following is based upon a true, Arch story.

If you're a fan of tall tales, here's a story that's extra-large.
It's about the time my family and I went to visit the Gateway Arch.

We went all the way to the top, where the view was amazing to see.

But I couldn't help but get the feeling that something else was watching me!

The next morning I awoke to a rustling sound outside.
I went to the window and that's when my eyes got wide.

8

You'll never believe what I saw standing in my front yard alone.
It was the Arch, the St. Louis Arch! It had followed me home!

9

I tiptoed outside, still not sure I was awake.
That's when the Arch leaned over and gave my hand a gentle shake.

"What an imagination!" my parents exclaimed when I told them about our guest.
But they stopped laughing when the Arch decided to join us for breakfast.

Later that morning I left for school, and the Arch came along as well.

My teacher fainted when I introduced him during show and tell.

13

We never did find the soccer ball that the Arch kicked on the playground outside.

But he made up for it by turning himself into the perfect recess slide.

On a field trip to a baseball game, the Arch couldn't stay away.
He took up an entire section of seats and boy, did he love doing the wave.

After the game, we made new friends at one of the city's great dog parks.

We even had time to play cowboy before it began to get dark.

The very next morning I awoke figuring the Arch was now long gone.
But he had returned, and the Arch had brought some of his friends along.

There was a statue of "Stan, the Man," always ready for a ballgame.

Stan was sharing a laugh with the statue of Louis the 14th and the King from the Chess Hall of Fame.

20

We spotted the Dog Town turtles and the statues of Lewis and Clark,

And Citygarden's Pinocchio and that eye ball from Laumeier Park.

I saw the Botanical Garden's dancing fairies and a big bottle of *Vess* soda pop.

And there was the giant praying mantis from the City Museum rooftop.

24

The T-Rex from the Science Center sat on the Kirkwood sculpture of chairs.

And inside the giant high-heeled shoe were the Peabody Opera House bears.

Not to mention those steel animal sculptures from the St. Louis Zoo.
They were hanging out with the monarch from the Butterfly House, there too.

They were all there. Every statue and landmark. Every St. Louis gem.

And they just wanted to have fun with me. And I couldn't disappoint them.

That day we did a little of everything, as we toured every inch of the Lou.

I took them on a float trip. Some could barely fit in a raft or canoe.

I took them to the National Blues Museum, which brought huge smiles to the group.

And then we hopped a trolley car bound for the Walk of Fame on the Loop.

While I was out having adventures with all my new friends,
The rest of the city was now empty, where those landmarks had been.

34

"There they are!" called a little girl. The crowd said, "Go ahead! Lead on!"
And the little girl led the crowd to all the landmarks on my front lawn.

"Please," the girl said to me. "I know you've had a wonderful day,
But without all those landmarks, St. Louis just isn't the same."

36

"We need them. They teach and inspire us. Our history, they prolong.
So would it be okay if they all went back to where they belong?"

We all knew she was right. I looked up at my brand new friend.
He gave my shoulder a nudge and disappeared with the wind.

They all went back, but as each returned to his and her own neck of the woods,
They each gave me a wave, and I knew that today had been something good.

39

When I tell you that my tale is true, you might roll your eyes and groan,
But let me ask you, what would you do, if the Arch followed you home?

Who's Who of Landmarks in the Lou

**The Gateway Arch
- The Arch Grounds**

"I tend to look down on Chicago sports fans."

**Man on a Horse
- Clayton**

"We ran over eleven lawyers today. Good day."

**Tyrannosaurus Rex
- The St. Louis Science Center**

"I'm actually a T-Rav-osaurus Rex."

**Dancing Fairies
- The Missouri Botantical Garden**

"Come February, we high tail it for the Climatron."

**Dog Town Turtles
- Dog Town**

"Kiss us, we're Irish!"

**Brooks Catsup Bottle Water Tower
- Collinsville, IL**

"You ever see an order of french fries the size of a Chevy, let me know."

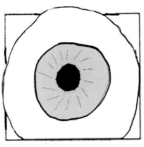

Eye
-Laumeier Sculpture Park

"I'm winking at you!
Cha, cha, cha..."

Thinker on a Rock
-Washington University

"Frozen custard or
gooey butter cake? Hmmm."

King Louis IX
- Forest Park

"Holding this sword by the
blade. Not my best idea."

Praying Mantis
- The City Museum

"I eat bugs and small
aircraft."

Shoe of Shoes
- Brown Shoe Company

"You'll never believe
how much shoe polish
I go through in a month."

Bird
-Citygarden

"Even I'm not sure what
the heck I really am."

About the Author and Illustrator

Ryan Nusbickel is an Emmy-winning former St. Louis television reporter, who went to the top of the Arch and then, subsequently, lost to the Arch in a game of washers.

Nusbickel has written and illustrated five other books for young people, including *Cloudy With A Chance of Toasted Rav, "Who Moved My Gooey Butter Cake?!," The St. Louis Night Before Christmas,* and *The St. Louis 12 Days of Christmas.*

He lives in St Louis with his wife, Margaret, and daughters, Genevieve and Caroline, who would like the Arch to join their next tea party.

You can visit him online at nusbickelbooks.com, twitter, and Facebook.

The author/illustrator interviewing the Arch in preparation for this book. *Picture by Marz and Gabriele Ratynksi from Chicago, who happened to be walking by.*

Make your high school proud. Collect all of Ryan's books.

It's the Night Before Christmas (with gooey butter cake.)

Giant slingers dump chili on Cub fans. You're welcome.

"The book for the St. Louisan who has everything."
-FEAST MAGAZINE

Because Christmas in St. Louis is too much fun for just one day!

All of Ryan's books can be purchased at over fifty area retailers and on his website: www.nusbickelbooks.com.

Made in the USA
San Bernardino, CA
26 September 2017